Shits and Giggles — Screw Burnout!

From exhaustion to empowerment:
Own your comeback.

By

Monya Maxwell

© 2024 Monya Maxwell

All rights reserved.

No part of this book may be reproduced, distributed, or transmitted in any form or by any means, including photocopying, recording, or other electronic or mechanical methods, without the prior written permission of the publisher, except in the case of brief quotations embodied in critical reviews and certain other non-commercial uses permitted by copyright law.

ISBN: 978-1-0370-2460-3

First Edition: November 2024

Published by Monya Maxwell

Contents

Introduction 1
My Experience with Burnout 3
What is Burnout? 11
The Next Step 17
Understanding Stress 25
Statistics 35
What to Do 39
    Vitality 42
    Daily Priming and Visualisation 46
    Letting Go of Emotions 53
    Focus Time 58
    Yoga Nidra 60
    Meditation 63
    Exercise 66
    Talk Therapy 69
    Healthy Diet 72
    Breathwork 73
Anhedonia 77
About the Author 85
Reference list 87

Introduction

The reason I started writing this book is simple: I had to deal with burnout. Actually, I was beyond burnout. For years, I bounced between fight or flight. And then, eventually, I hit freeze. I'm talking literal freeze—like playing dead. I watched my life fall apart, unable to get up and do anything about it.

It took me 20 years to stop and look at this thing called burnout, to truly understand it, to handle it. When I thought it was a ball of play-dough, I could just mould and shape it into what I wanted it to be. Thinking I could control it.

In this book, I look at different aspects of burnout, what it is, where it comes from, some statistics (we can not create a book on research without some good old stats) and how to deal with it.

This book is not written with any specific religion or spiritual beliefs in mind. There are various methods which aid in dealing with stress. Whether it is the more mechanical techniques based on science, or whether you prefer to embrace the more religious or spiritual route, or the psychological mindfulness route. See what you resonate with and use those methods. If you are open and willing to try something different, then that is your prerogative. And if you only choose to stick with what you know or is in your comfort zone, then that too works. I believe it is our soul's purpose to grow and evolve as individuals.

My Experience with Burnout

Ever since I can remember, I have been busy. By the time I wrote this book, I had experienced burnout three times—or, let me rephrase that, I went through three episodes in my life of dealing with great fatigue. Not that it is actually great. It sucks!

I am the person who is always busy with something. Well, I used to be, and I am still a work in progress, learning to relax and to say "no." There is a statement that says "No." is a full sentence. As simple as it sounds, it is not always easy to do. Especially if you are a people pleaser. Gratefully, I am a well-recovered people pleaser. Thank goodness for that!

But even during a simple thing like watching TV or sitting at a family braai, I used to be busy knitting, crocheting, or shooting stuff up with the glue gun (you would be amazed how you can suddenly find things to glue together just for the sake of being busy). It is a curse to be highly organised and efficient. Even my clutter used to be organised. Being organised does sound intriguing, like something everyone should achieve – a life goal. But the truth is, not knowing how or even when to stop and relax is a problem! It is like an addiction.

"Hi, I am Monya. I am an always-busy-with-something addict."

What is the point of it all? For me, it was about the need to achieve. I needed to feel like I was doing something productive, adding value (but to whom?). And how much of it really paid off? Was any of it even worth it? Sometimes I look back and wonder, what did I really achieve? Don't get me wrong, I am still a driven person, with a bit more balance in life.

There was this one time my photography studio neighbour, who is a seamstress (and she makes the most delicate and exquisite dresses), gave me two big boxes of cut-off fabrics. I was over the moon with excitement! Straight away, I got to work and made make-do outfits for my studio maternity sessions (don't be fooled by the beautiful, elegant dresses you might see in some photos. When it's in the studio, there is a good chance it is just a piece of fabric tied up in a creative way to make it look like a dress. This is what I mean by creating make-do outfits, as most of my maternity sessions at that time were done in my studio). I was stitching up every free minute for months, close to a year. My outfit collection grew five times larger. Towards the end, I had to install an extra well-supported rail for all these outfits to carry the weight. And then, another year later, I started selling some of these outfits, gave some away, and even chucked some in the bin because there were just too many outfits for my clients to choose from, or it was unpopular colours. Most of those hours spent sewing were for nothing! But I liked being busy.

Okay, yes - through a lot of the "being busy" moments, I did learn how to improve my business by setting up websites, doing my own SEO, and making my own props. All for the sake of saving some money. In all fairness, it is not always viable to outsource some tasks when the budget does not allow it, because you are a small one-person business. You must put the time and effort into knowing the industry and how to get the basics set up for your business, along with managing the accounting side. Given that we are human, we tend to learn through trial and error. You can quite easily spend four to six hours just learning the best practices to set up social media ads before you even create the first ad.

It boils down to honesty. Looking back, I realised there were times I got so caught up in figuring things out that I did not take time to calm the f*ck down and just breathe. Take a step back, say it is enough for today, and just let your brain process all the information consumed. In hindsight, I did waste time on pointless busyness. Sometimes in our unproductive state, we have convinced ourselves we are super productive. There were easier and simpler solutions, or I just went with something without thinking it through properly, because I liked being busy. By taking a moment to step aside and just process, I could have done some things a bit better, which in the end would have produced better results and taken less time. But I liked being busy.

When you are in that rut to just achieve and succeed, it can be difficult to take a moment to sit still for 15 minutes and just f*cking relax. Just breathe! Note to self (and you, dear reader): I found something beautiful called YogaNidra. A simple 15-minute script can reset your energy like you had several hours of deep restful sleep.

The first time I dealt with burnout was shortly after I started my first corporate job. Now, I come from a low-income household where I was a waitress during my last school years, so I could afford to buy my own toiletries and clothing, and there were no funds to study. I continued working as a waitress after school, not sure what I wanted to become. When your life makes you feel small, like you are not included in the opportunities bucket, it can be difficult to try to figure out what you want to do with your life (the apathy emotion – mental note, as this will be discussed later). What is the point of choosing a line when you feel you are not even allowed to stand in the line? My grades were not good enough for university. I just missed the mark. And even if it was, there was no financial backing. Home life was not supportive enough to help me figure out my gifts, passion, or talents. The unspoken expectation was to just get a job, any job, and work hard. Just work hard! That is the only option for people like us. So, I just went with the motions.

Starting my first office job in a small corporate company, I was dedicated. I was given an opportunity, and I worked with passion like it were my own company. Unknowingly, that was also what they wanted: that naive, over-committed dedication. Not long after, the saying in the office was that if you want something done, give it to Monya. And Monya just said yes. She (aka me) was the jack of all trades (master of none) and just so willing to do things for a little recognition.

Gosh, I was in my early twenties when the doctor diagnosed me with "burnout" and prescribed me antidepressants, escorted me out of the room, and grabbed his next patient's file. Okay, now what? The pills are supposed to fix this thing called "burnout". I had never even heard of it before. It is not something you can see or touch. It was not like I had a rash I could see or even a pounding headache I could feel. I was just exhausted and felt unmotivated and deflated. And he prescribed me antidepressants! At that stage of my life, I thought depression was something you went to a psychologist for, for people who feel suicidal or who have serious problems. I had no clue what depression or burnout was.

Back at the office, life went on as usual. There was no support or concern about the doctor's note. All my manager told me was that I needed to be careful of antidepressants as they can have side effects and become addictive. And that was it. Good advice, I was grateful for, but still no help in dealing with the burnout. They needed their jack of all trades back at her desk (and yes, I was a very willing participant; I felt valued). Yet, still, I did not quite understand what the heck "burnout" was or take any steps to deal with it. Even though I had access to the internet, I did not think to research it. My to-do list was waiting, and people looked at me to see how quickly I would pick up the pace again. In my view, they relied on me, and I could not let them down. And just like that, life went on, and I just went with the punches.

Years went on with corporate struggles, exhaustion, struggling to regulate my mood, feelings of depression and anxiety, with my cortisol levels, and at times, this agonising headache that felt like someone was stabbing my eye out from inside my skull. And it just kept going and going and going. I had a bad appetite and struggled to gain weight (yes, gain. I looked like a vacuum-packed skeleton, even though I am a petite build. I was very underweight). Coffee and chocolates were my staple diet.

Several years later, dealing with a terribly stressful divorce pushed me close to the edge, where I felt I could collapse standing in the grocery line. There were days I think people thought I was drunk because I felt so disorientated from tiredness. One day, I remember nearly falling asleep standing in line at the local grocery store. If people asked me how I was doing, my automated response was "I am good, just tired". And for years, I thought this was okay. Maybe even normal. My life was busy, of course, I was going to be tired. After all, I am just tired. It is normal, isn't it? "No one has died from it." Looking back at that statement now, people do die from exhaustion: falling asleep while driving or working in factories with equipment, where there are physical injuries.

Finally, at the end of last year, it hit me again, hard! I remember days when I could barely get up. I would sit the whole day on the chair outside on the patio. Not even able to read a book or watch TV. The idea of binge-watching Netflix even felt like work, and exhausting. My brain, my mind, my body, and my soul were drained! And yet still, I did not know what burnout was, nor could I even admit it.

Remember, I'm a busy person, and a busy person is tired. That was how I saw things.

How can we deal with a problem if we cannot even face it or understand it? It has been 20 years for me, and I do hope it does not take that long for you to understand and recover.

Fortunately, during most of this, I have been healthy. The occasional flu, colds, and runny nose. I have always told myself and people that I am a healthy person (and when it comes to mindset, I am thankful I developed this healthy habit of always being healthy). Others dealing with burnout were not so lucky. Some people have reported serious health troubles, and some even struggled to get a proper medical diagnosis and effective treatment. When your body is severely tired, burnout can manifest in several different ways. Because it is not like a vitamin C deficiency, many doctors do not know how to diagnose it, leading to ineffective treatment (at least this was my experience over the years of Doctor's visits, the few I had). A healthy, balanced lifestyle is our responsibility, after all.

It has been 20 years for me riding these waves of burnout before I had the courage to call it quits. I do hope it does not take that long for you to understand and recover.

Now, let us look at what burnout means.

What is Burnout?

What the f*ck is "burnout"? After all, it is not like we are physically on fire or feeling any burning sensations – unless you have serious muscle spasms, which can feel like a muscle on fire. Is burnout even a medical term? Neuroscientists talk about it as severe fatigue. When we think about the word "burnout", we can relate it to a candle burning out. However, we are not candles that can be replaced with a new one when we burn out. Then again, your boss might think differently. When a person quits their job, the hunt starts for the next replacement. The sad truth about life, I suppose.

We don't physically burn out, which also means we can come back from this thing called burnout or, more accurately, severe fatigue. I am not talking about the reincarnation way of coming back. You can recover physically, mentally and emotionally. Like me, you might even be in denial of being burned out. Or you kind of admit it to yourself in secret, but do not have the courage to admit it to family or a close friend or even a stranger, not daring to say it out loud or even in a whisper.

Herbert Freudenberger coined the original technical definition of burnout in the 1970s, and he added three components to it:

Depersonalisation: Separating yourself emotionally from your work instead of investing in it, where you feel it is meaningful.

Decreased sense of accomplishment: Working harder and harder while feeling that what you are doing is making less and less of a difference. (I can completely relate here!).

Emotional exhaustion. (A lot of women struggle here.)

Each of us experiences "burnout" in a different way. Men tend to feel more of a lack of meaning, and women tend to feel more emotionally exhausted.

Farber identifies three distinct types of burnout: wear out, classic burnout, and underchallenged burnout. In wear out, a person becomes exhausted and eventually gives up, feeling drained from constant stress. Classic burnout describes those who push themselves harder and harder in response to stress, often to the point of severe exhaustion. Lastly, underchallenged burnout happens when individuals face not overwhelming stress but rather dull, unstimulating conditions, leaving them disengaged and unmotivated. Each type reflects a different way of reacting to workplace stress, yet they all lead to the same endpoint—feeling burned out and detached. "Burnout" sucks! You feel lost, yet you know exactly where you are in the physical world. Sometimes you can feel excited and depressed at the same time. Life is great but also sh*t at the same time. How can this be? You accomplished this and that, yet you feel drained and like life is upside down with no gravity.

I often listen to Dr Andrew Huberman's podcast, a prominent neuroscientist, and he has discussed the topic of stress in detail. Stress is not our enemy. It is important to understand stress and how it can be useful, in the right dose. All traumas, anxiety, and fears map back to stress in some way (perhaps an area of self-exploration here, for later). Stress can have both positive and negative effects depending on how it is perceived and managed. Huberman emphasises that stress, when approached with the right mindset, can enhance performance, improve cognitive function, and lead to better health outcomes.

Further to this, Huberman explains that viewing stress as a challenge rather than a threat can lead to positive physiological responses, such as increased blood oxygenation and better problem-solving abilities. This mindset can also reduce inflammation and slow ageing. Stress can improve cognitive abilities, boost performance, and even have beneficial effects on cell ageing when managed properly. By understanding and harnessing the potential benefits of stress, individuals can transform it into a tool for growth and improvement. This involves recognising stressors as opportunities for adaptation and learning rather than mere threats, leading to increased well-being and elevated performance. Athletes are great examples of optimising stress to improve performance and reach their goals. Richard Sutton is also an expert in the field of stress and athletic performance and has written several books on this.

What is burnout? Stress. Chronic stress.

Huberman further discusses burnout as a multifaceted issue primarily arising from chronic stress and excessive workload. He describes burnout as being closely associated with "too much adrenaline, lack of sleep, and feeling both tired and wired." Burnout isn't just about the quantity of work but also the type of work and the constant administrative overhead that can lead to a feeling of disengagement and exhaustion. The feeling of burnout can be mitigated by embracing "wholeheartedness," or fully engaging in work with genuine interest and passion. This approach contrasts with the fragmented attention often required in modern workplaces, where frequent meetings and constant emails can make individuals feel like they are always talking about work rather than doing it.

Stress in itself is not evil. Only when you have a too high dosage over a too long period of time.

Being overwhelmingly exhausted is your body sounding the alarm bells loudly to indicate the imbalance and misalignment in your life. As much as parts of your life are great, there are parts that need serious attention and redirection. The only way to get it is to STOP. It is okay to feel this way. It's okay to stop. We will discuss methods later in the book.

"Wait, what? No, I have deadlines! I have no choice! I cannot stop! Bills! This and that need to be sorted out first!". All the excuses will drag you further down. The further down you fall, the harder it is to climb back up. I did not say you will not get back up because you will. Most people who suffer from "burnout" are overachievers. One thing we f*cking rock at is getting back up and facing challenges! Because we are fighters, we are determined, but we are also extremely exhausted.

If you want something done, give it to a busy person...

Exhaustion is a normal thing. It is something we all experience – overachiever or not. We all feel it at some point. But it is what we do when we feel it is something that we need to address. Do we ignore it and think, "Ag, it's not that bad. I will rest tomorrow, next week, next month, next year, when I'm dead?".

"I will sleep when I'm dead" – that is a shitty quote or motto. Get rid of that crap – fast!

The descent into burnout is fast, but the recovery is slow. But because we are not burned-out candles, but rather fatigued humans, recovery is possible. I keep repeating this, in the hope it sinks in. You will not come to an end if you crash! We try to get as much done before we know we are about to crash, in the fear that we will not get up. But I think if we understood that we can and will recover, we would not push so hard and fall so far down. This also means that if you fall only a little, you get back up faster.

The American Psychological Association defines burnout as emotional, mental, or physical exhaustion accompanied by decreased motivation, lower performance, and negative attitudes toward oneself and others. The result of performing at a high level until stress and tension take their toll.

We outrun ourselves, we outdo ourselves, but not in a good way. Testing our limits is good, but breaking yourself in the process is not worth it. We will look at suggested practical tools to manage and prevent burnout, such as stress inoculation techniques, breathing exercises, and mindfulness practices. These tools aim to help individuals control their stress in real-time and avoid the long-term negative effects of chronic stress and burnout.

After Freudenberger, a psychologist in New York in the 1970s, broke down from burnout, he started an in-depth self-study. In his published paper, he asked, "Who is prone to burnout?" to which he unequivocally stated: "The dedicated and the committed."

We will not care so much what people think about us when we realise how little they think about us in the first place.

Let that sink in for a moment.

The Next Step

Before we explore different techniques to deal with and recover from burnout, we first need to understand how we got here in the first place. Identifying and breaking the pattern is essential, or you'll keep repeating it, as I did. If you feel tempted to skip this chapter and head straight to the solution, please make sure to come back. It might be uncomfortable, but it's crucial for finding and maintaining balance. Fixing burnout isn't about quick fixes or magic pills; it requires work to rewire new patterns and belief in your life, and often to deal with unresolved trauma.

Understanding the "why" might take time. Humans often struggle to be honest with themselves, making self-reflection difficult, uncomfortable, and time-consuming. After reading this chapter, you'll need to start the work, which you can do alongside the cure. However, don't think the cure alone will fix you. It is like saying to an addict, to be healthy, they can continue using their poison as long as they follow a healthy diet. It does not work.

For many, the root cause stems back to our childhood. Yes, the good old days of playing ring-a-rosy, falling off the slide, learning to ride your bike, and playing with squeaky toys in the bath. It might sound taboo (here comes the psychologist with childhood trauma crap! "I'm a grown man, not a crying three-year-old. Spare me the pity party crap, Monya!"). But indulge me and listen to what others have to say.

Our lives are created on patterns and beliefs formed during our childhood, both good and bad. Some refer to this as our framework—the habits ingrained in us, like making your bed as soon as you wake up or that aversion to peas because your father was allergic. Or that weird thing you have done ever since you can remember. These patterns shape our behaviours and responses.

Have you watched Tony Robbins in one of his live shows (or the documentary on Netflix) where he talks to someone from the audience? He often asks about their relationship with their parents and which parent's love they craved the most. Then he asks, "Who did you need to be for that parent?" The answers often reveal deep-rooted issues, like the need to be perfect or to impress your parents, which can lead to constantly feeling inadequate and pushing hard at something meaningless to you. This could be the reason or belief which is causing the burnout. These stories need reevaluating or rewriting.

I think for people struggling with burnout, the need to be perfect, excel, impress your parents, give them bragging rights, being the eldest child who had to look after the younger siblings, or what other child you had to be for them, is deeply ingrained in our stories of who we are. These stories are often the leading cause of constantly feeling not enough, to push hard at something which does not hold meaning to us personally. It causes us to question our worth and what we can do to make ourselves worthy, accepted, relied upon, and feel valued.

For some, it means taking up a specific career because it's expected, or, like me, floating along in a job, working hard for the next promotion, but finding it all meaningless. We need purpose and meaning in our daily lives, including our careers. Not having meaningful work can make us feel stuck.

Do you really enjoy your job? Perhaps you're overworked, with long hours and too many tasks, leaving your brain overstimulated. If you like your job despite feeling drained, ask yourself what you like about it and how it makes a difference. Are we honest when we say we love our jobs, or do we secretly daydream about something else? This job might not be bad, with good benefits, great colleagues and a family to support, but something might still pull at your heartstrings.

That pull might be something you daydream about but feel too scared to explore. It stirs a bit of excitement, makes you feel excited and enthusiastic, a desire to express yourself, and offers more meaning to your life.

Not having meaningful work can make a person feel stuck.

I once read a phrase that was my email signature for years, but I struggled to apply it to my life:

"Don't ask yourself what the world needs. Ask yourself what makes you come alive, and go do that, because what the world needs is people who have come alive."

I'm still unsure if I've found what makes me feel alive, and it might change through different life stages. When I started my photography business, it was for me. It gave me independence and basic business skills, the courage to create my own style, speak up for myself, step out of my comfort zone, and ultimately helped me rebuild my life after a failed marriage. It was my bridge to doing something different and making a bigger impact in my personal life. And I did it starting from scratch, without borrowing money.

I'm not saying quit your job and figure it out. Instead, ask yourself if you have a sense of purpose. We all need purpose; it's the foundation of personal growth and a great life.

Carl Jung explored the human psyche, and he defined the shadow self. And some might have heard the term "shadow work". It might sound crazy, scary or even witchy, but I promise it has nothing to do with potions and spells ☺ (Am I allowed to put smiley faces in a book? I don't know, I am new at being an Author – haha. Never as a child would I have thought to write anything like a blog or even a book! I did not even read books!).

Okay, back on track with the shadow self.

Carl Jung explored the human psyche and defined the shadow self. The shadow self represents the unconscious part of the personality, containing traits and desires we find undesirable or socially unacceptable. Jung believed that acknowledging and integrating the shadow is essential for achieving psychological wholeness. This process, known as individuation, involves bringing the unconscious aspects of the self into conscious awareness, leading to a more balanced and complete personality.

Embracing the shadow self allows for personal growth and self-acceptance, reducing internal conflicts and psychological tension. The shadow contains not only negative traits but also positive qualities that have been repressed. Integrating the shadow can unleash creativity, vitality, and untapped potential, contributing to a richer and more fulfilling life. I will admit, I am still a work in progress here.

The shadow is formed through the process of socialisation, where certain behaviours and impulses are deemed inappropriate or unacceptable and are thus pushed into the unconscious mind. This is why we behave differently in different social settings. No, you do not have a split personality. We just...want to be liked by others. So, we conform to the setting we find ourselves in.

Often, we project our shadow aspects onto others, attributing our undesirable traits to people around us. Recognising and integrating the shadow reduces this projection, leading to healthier relationships and a more accurate perception of others. Jung saw the shadow as a necessary and natural part of the human psyche, emphasising the importance of engaging with it to achieve a harmonious and integrated self. Balance! Understanding we are NOT perfect (even if you think the sun shines out your butt – you are still not perfect). We all have flaws and strengths, things we like about ourselves and things we do not. The bottom line is to understand the balance and accept ourselves.

The source of burnout is often a major misalignment in your life.

Understanding and accepting ourselves helps us live more authentically and wholeheartedly. Wholeheartedness involves engaging in life with authenticity, courage, and vulnerability, fully embracing our imperfections and living with a sense of worthiness, connection, and compassion. According to Brené Brown, wholehearted living includes cultivating qualities like gratitude, joy, resilience, and a sense of belonging.

Wholeheartedness can protect against burnout. When we live wholeheartedly, we're more likely to set healthy boundaries, practice self-care, and seek balance in our personal and professional lives. Embracing vulnerability and authenticity builds emotional resilience, helping us cope with stress and recover from setbacks. Wholehearted living fosters a sense of connection and community, providing emotional resources and practical assistance during challenging times. It helps us find purpose and meaning, buffering against the emptiness and exhaustion characteristic of burnout.

Consider burnout as a signpost to get back on track.

Living authentically reduces internal conflict from trying to meet external expectations at the expense of our true selves. This alignment between values and actions lowers stress levels and contributes to overall well-being. Being kind to ourselves and recognising our limits helps manage stress and avoid over-commitment.

Ask yourself this important question: "If I were to die right now, am I ready? If not, what lights me up, what gives me joy?" and then listen.

Understanding the dynamics of motivation is crucial in overcoming burnout. Tony Robbins' concept of "push versus pull" offers valuable insights. Push motivation is driven by external pressures, such as deadlines and societal expectations, often leading to stress and burnout. Pull motivation, however, is fueled by internal desires and passions. It involves being naturally drawn to goals that resonate with our values and interests, making actions feel more effortless and enjoyable. Aligning our goals with what excites us creates a sustainable source of energy and enthusiasm, reducing burnout and enhancing overall fulfilment.

Embracing pull motivation requires a mindset shift and a deeper understanding of our passions and values. Instead of forcing ourselves to meet external expectations, we should focus on activities that ignite our inner drive. This approach makes our work more enjoyable, fostering creativity and long-term satisfaction. By transitioning from a push to a pull motivation framework, we can achieve our goals with greater ease and joy, ultimately leading to a more balanced and fulfilling life.

This might sound easy and straightforward, and for some, it might be. They may already know what their passion is, and the light bulb has switched on for how to create a more meaningful life. But for others, like me, it's been more of an uphill struggle to figure out—and to still earn an income along the way. For some, this journey might lead to a career change, while for others, it could be as simple as dedicating one morning a week to community work. Dive deep, do some soul-searching, and take steps forward. You might not find the answer right away, but by taking action, you're shifting your perspective. And sometimes, that's all you need to see the horizon.

Understanding Stress

Is stress a friend or a foe?

Stress involves two key elements: stressors, which are the things that cause stress, and physiological stress, which is the body's reaction to a perceived threat. When we sense a threat, our body activates a "fight-or-flight" response, directing all energy toward survival. Cortisol, dopamine, and other hormones focus on this singular goal: avoid danger! The stress response cycle includes perceiving a threat, responding to it, and then signalling to the body that the potential threat has passed. This cycle indicates it is safe to relax. However, in modern times, we often fail to relax after stressful moments, meaning we do not complete the cycle. To help our bodies transition to a state of safety, engaging in physical activities like walking, doing jumping jacks, or tensing and then relaxing all our muscles can be beneficial. These actions help shift our physiological state to one of calm and security.

If you had a long and stressful day at the office and arrive home, after battling the traffic for an hour, try one of these methods to complete the stress cycle. It will alert your brain that you are back in a safe zone and can relax.

Burnout, while not a medical diagnosis or mental illness, is a condition resulting from overwhelming stress. It highlights the necessity of completing our stress response cycles. Stress is defined as the body's and brain's adaptive response to perceived threats or challenges. It encompasses a physiological and psychological state triggered by external or internal stimuli, known as stressors. Stress can manifest in emotional, physical, and cognitive responses and can be either acute (short-term) or chronic (long-term).

While burnout is not classified as a medical condition or mental illness, it is acknowledged as a significant occupational issue that can affect a person's mental and physical health. Therefore, it's essential for individuals experiencing burnout to seek support and implement strategies to manage stress and improve their well-being.

Stress is not all evil. It is the thing that gets us moving when we need to move, even fast!

The purpose of stress is to prepare the body to face challenges and threats. This "fight-or-flight" response involves physiological changes, such as increased heart rate, elevated blood pressure, and the release of stress hormones like adrenaline and cortisol. These changes enhance the body's ability to react quickly and effectively to immediate dangers, aiding in survival. Stress also contributes to learning and adaptation, motivating individuals to develop coping strategies to overcome challenges, and ultimately fostering personal growth and resilience.

Experiencing a small, regular amount of stress can have a positive effect on the immune system by acting as a stimulus that prompts the body's defences to remain active and responsive. This type of stress, often referred to as "eustress" or "positive stress," can enhance the immune system's efficiency by:

> Boosting Immune Function: Mild stressors can stimulate the production of immune cells, such as natural killer cells and T-cells, which play a crucial role in defending the body against pathogens and infections.
>
> Preparing the Body for Challenges: Regular exposure to manageable stress can help the body adapt and respond more effectively to future stressors, promoting resilience and an enhanced ability to cope with more severe stress.
>
> Maintaining Homeostasis: The body's stress response, when activated in moderation, can help maintain a balanced internal environment, allowing for better regulation of bodily functions, including the immune system.
>
> Promoting Adaptation and Growth: Like how muscles grow stronger with regular exercise, the immune system can become more robust and adaptive through exposure to mild stress, preparing the body to handle more significant challenges.

However, it is crucial to distinguish between beneficial, mild stress and chronic, overwhelming stress. While the former can enhance immune function and overall well-being, the latter can lead to detrimental health effects, including a weakened immune system, increased susceptibility to illnesses, and other health issues. Thus, managing stress effectively and ensuring it remains at a beneficial level is key to supporting overall health and well-being.

A simple definition of burnout is feeling overwhelmed and exhausted by everything we do, with the sense that it is never enough. When we can't get out of bed or complete basic tasks, this is beyond burnout. Burnout is characterised by still managing to get up and go to work, but constantly daydreaming about a different job or place. It stems from our inability to acknowledge the difficulties building up inside. The solution lies in turning towards these challenging feelings with kindness and acceptance. Feelings are like tunnels; we need to go through them to reach the light at the end. Avoid getting stuck in the middle or fearing our uncomfortable internal emotions.

Even though a lot has been said about self-care, it is crucial to understand that self-care alone is not a complete solution to burnout or stress. While engaging in self-care activities such as exercise, relaxation, or hobbies can offer temporary relief, they do not address the underlying issues that contribute to burnout. To truly recover and maintain well-being, we need more than just individual efforts; we need a supportive network of people around us.

Self-care often emphasises individual resilience and independence, suggesting that by strengthening ourselves, we can overcome challenges on our own.

However, this perspective can be misleading. The reality is that no one is an island, and attempting to handle everything alone can lead to further isolation and stress. Instead, the concept of interdependence—recognising the importance of mutual support and connection with others—plays a crucial role in overall well-being. Self-care is not a solution. We need a bubble of love from people to help us. It is not about being stronger and independent – we need interdependence, it is higher than independence.

Interdependence involves building and nurturing relationships where both giving and receiving support are valued. It means reaching out for help when needed and offering support to others. This mutual exchange creates a web of support that can help us navigate life's difficulties more effectively. It allows us to share burdens, celebrate successes together, and find comfort and strength in the community.

Rather than focusing solely on becoming stronger and more independent, embracing interdependence acknowledges that we thrive in a network of relationships. By fostering meaningful connections and allowing ourselves to rely on and support others, we create a more balanced and resilient approach to managing stress and preventing burnout. Thus, interdependence not only enhances our capacity to cope with challenges but also enriches our overall quality of life.

Dr David R. Hawkins, known for his work in psychiatry and spiritual teachings, discussed stress in the context of consciousness and emotional well-being. He viewed stress as a response arising from lower levels of consciousness, often tied to negative emotions and perceptions. According to Hawkins, stress results from an individual's attachment to outcomes, fears, and unresolved emotions. He emphasised the importance of letting go of these attachments and fears to achieve higher states of consciousness and emotional freedom. In his book *Letting Go: The Pathway of Surrender*, Hawkins suggests that by surrendering to the present moment and releasing the need for control, individuals can reduce stress and experience a more peaceful and harmonious state of being. This approach aligns with his broader teachings on emotional healing and spiritual enlightenment, where releasing negative emotions and thoughts leads to inner peace and reduced stress.

If you're more interested in the scientific side of stress, I highly recommend reading *The Stress Code – From Surviving to Thriving* by Richard Sutton. He's an expert in stress management who works with athletes and provides business coaching. His books explore the topic of stress in great detail and offer practical insights backed by science.

People often blame those experiencing burnout for having a maladaptive response to stress—an accusation I once faced from a former boss. Burnout can make people feel less human and more like robots. While PTSD and burnout have distinct origins and definitions, they share similarities that provide insight into their management and treatment. Recognising these parallels is crucial for developing effective strategies for those affected by either condition.

Emotional Exhaustion: Both PTSD and burnout can result in profound emotional fatigue. Individuals with PTSD may experience a range of emotional responses, from numbness to intense feelings, while those facing burnout often feel emotionally drained, detached, and depleted.

Cognitive Difficulties: Cognitive impairments are common in both conditions. PTSD sufferers might struggle with concentration, memory, and decision-making, hindered by intrusive thoughts and a state of hyperarousal. Similarly, burnout can lead to decreased concentration, forgetfulness, and diminished critical thinking due to prolonged mental fatigue.

Avoidance Behaviours: Avoidance is a coping mechanism in both PTSD and burnout. Individuals with PTSD might steer clear of anything associated with their trauma, while those with burnout often avoid work-related tasks or social interactions, driven by a lack of motivation or energy.

Physical Symptoms: The physical manifestations of PTSD and burnout are notable. PTSD can present hyperarousal symptoms, such as increased heart rate and heightened startle responses. Burnout can cause physical ailments like headaches, gastrointestinal issues, and sleep disturbances stemming from chronic stress.

Impact on Relationships: Both conditions can strain relationships, both personal and professional. PTSD can lead to withdrawal or irritability, impacting interactions with loved ones. Those experiencing burnout might feel isolated, cynical, or disengaged from colleagues, friends, and family.

By examining and understanding our fears, we can then choose a different path.

A study was done among university students during the COVID-19 pandemic. It looked at how existential anxiety and academic fear impact the relationship between academic burnout and PTSD symptoms among university students.

The pandemic heightened concerns about life's meaning, personal existence, and the fragility of life. In the study, it is noted, trauma can deeply affect a person's view of the world, their self-perception, and their place in the world. For students, past traumas combined with new challenges, such as transitioning to online learning and dealing with inadequate resources and support, worsened their fears and stresses. This environment led to increased existential anxiety and academic fears, which in turn escalated burnout and traumatic experiences.

The study's findings showed that students facing burnout, existential anxiety, and academic fears were at a higher risk for traumatic symptoms. While trauma can manifest differently and with varying severity, the research highlighted educational stressors beyond bullying that may elevate PTSD symptoms. Recovery for students with traumatic experiences involved rebuilding life's meaning, self-identity, and confidence in academic abilities, alongside managing stress.

The holistic model for treating PTSD focuses on strengthening the body and mind to achieve balance. Everyone's experience of trauma is unique; while some may recover easily, others may develop PTSD. Assigning personal meaning to traumatic experiences is key, as Freud observed, where discussing and understanding the traumatic event helps alleviate symptoms. Others might say that finding meaning in a traumatic situation could cause a person to remain in a victim mindset, which is not an ideal state. Perhaps the best course of action would be to look at Dr Hawkins's method of letting go of emotions (which includes fear, guilt, shame and apathy – the negative emotions).

Statistics

Alright, let's talk about stats. It's only natural to look at some numbers as we go through this journey— maybe you'll realise you're not alone. Even though I knew I wasn't the first person to experience burnout, when my life felt like it was falling apart, it seemed as if I was the only one struggling.

Karen Curry Parker, a transformational teacher, speaker, coach, and author, conducted a survey with her newsletter subscribers, high-achieving individuals who value personal growth. Out of 1,000 respondents, she found that:

97% struggled with low self-worth,

92% had experienced some form of trauma,

87% experienced burnout, with some unable to go to work because of it.

According to Harvard Medicine, unresolved trauma is a leading cause of low self-worth and motivation. Parker defines trauma as any experience that causes us to lose our sense of value and awareness of our unique gifts. Trauma isn't limited to extreme incidents; even seemingly minor experiences, like not receiving support from family, can deeply impact our sense of self.

In her TEDx talk, A Better Job Won't Help – The Truth about Burnout, Karen Parker explores deeper causes of burnout beyond overwork. She highlights unresolved trauma, misalignment with one's true self, and disconnection from purpose as significant contributors. Burnout isn't just a workplace issue—it can impact caregiving, parenting, relationships, and personal ambitions.

Workplace Burnout:

A 2022 Gallup study found that 36% of South African workers experience extreme daily stress, while over 71% feel disengaged or actively disengaged at work—clear indicators of widespread burnout. The World Health Organisation (WHO) now classifies workplace burnout as an "occupational phenomenon," acknowledging its global mental health impact. In 2020, burnout levels reached unprecedented highs, with 43% of people in over 100 countries reporting workplace burnout (Global Workplace Burnout Report).

Caregiver Burnout:

A 2021 report by the National Alliance for Caregiving found that 23% of adult caregivers reported high-stress levels, with 40% experiencing emotional strain and 18% dealing with physical health issues due to caregiving demands.

Parental Burnout:

A 2020 study published in Frontiers in Psychology revealed that 5-12% of parents experience parental burnout, often leading to emotional detachment from their children and feelings of inadequacy. The American Psychological Association warns that burnout in parents can lead to neglect, self-doubt, and even thoughts of escape or abandonment. In Six Ways to Deal with Parental Burnout, Kendra Wilde shares her own experience with severe stress-related health problems, which she later identified as burnout. Wilde offers strategies like practising self-care, accepting parenting's inherent challenges, and letting go of the "perfect parent" ideal. She emphasises the importance of community support, suggesting that parents build their own "village" to help them cope. Seeking professional help is essential too; sometimes, severe burnout requires more than self-care alone. I can personally attest to this. If only I'd sought help sooner, maybe things wouldn't have spiralled as they did. Freezing up and watching everything collapse is terrifying. Reach out—speak up!

Relationship Burnout:

Though less widely studied, relationship burnout is still significant. According to a 2021 Journal of Marriage and Family study, 29% of married couples experience burnout, leading to emotional distancing and a decline in intimacy. Relationship burnout is marked by emotional exhaustion, frustration, and a sense of disconnection. Recognising these feelings is often the first step toward healing. Strategies like open communication, balancing personal and shared needs, and prioritising self-care can help revive the connection. Couples may also benefit from professional support, such as online therapy, to address the roots of burnout. By acknowledging the signs and taking proactive steps, couples can work to preserve and strengthen their relationships.

Academic Burnout:

The 2022 National College Health Assessment (NCHA) survey showed that 60% of students experienced overwhelming anxiety, while 40% felt so depressed it was hard to function. This mental strain often leads to academic burnout, marked by exhaustion, lack of motivation, and feelings of inadequacy, especially in high-stakes environments.

Burnout is a complex, pervasive issue that extends beyond the workplace, touching all areas of life. Whether you're a parent, caregiver, partner, or student, understanding burnout's causes and effects is the first step toward healing. Recognising these struggles in ourselves and others can remind us that we're not alone. Seeking support, aligning with our true values, and taking proactive steps can help us find our way back to resilience. Remember, recovery is possible—and you deserve it.

What to Do

There's an old saying I heard a lot as a child: "Too much of anything is not good." And we've already discussed stress. When stress keeps building up, unchecked and unresolved, it becomes trapped energy, bouncing around until it often leads to depression or even burnout.

There's no quick fix for burnout, and if you're feeling beyond burnt out, I genuinely wish you luck. The first step is simply to recognise it. The main goal is to restore a sense of vitality and purpose—or at least, that was my goal, and I found that others shared the same aim as I researched. Below, I've outlined several methods to manage stress and find a way forward.

Each person's journey with burnout is unique, and there isn't enough time in the day to try every suggestion at once. Start with what resonates most with you, taking each step when it feels right.

Recognise the Signs

The journey to recovery starts with understanding what burnout looks like in your life. Look for common signs like emotional exhaustion, feelings of ineffectiveness, or a sense of detachment. The sooner you recognise burnout, the sooner you can start to address it.

Accept Where You Are

It's natural to feel frustrated or even guilty for not coping better, but accepting your current state can actually be freeing. Acknowledging burnout is an act of courage, not weakness, and it can help you begin the healing process.

Set Boundaries

Boundaries protect your time and energy, which are crucial for recovery. Saying no to extra work, limiting certain obligations, or simply creating "you-time" can make a significant difference. Boundaries give you the space you need to rest and start healing.

Prioritise Self-Care

Self-care is often the first thing we neglect, but it's essential here. Prioritise activities that restore you—whether it's sleep, a relaxing hobby, or a short mindfulness practice each day. Self-care is not selfish; it's survival.

Seek Support

Burnout is hard to tackle alone. Talk to trusted friends, family, or colleagues, and don't hesitate to seek professional help if needed. The support of others can offer both comfort and practical resources as you start to rebuild.

Realign with Your Values

Often, burnout signals that something important in your life is out of sync with your core values. Take time to reflect on what truly matters to you, whether it's your career, relationships, or personal goals. Realigning your life to these values can help guide you forward.

Take Small Steps Toward Change

There's no need to overhaul everything overnight. Begin with small, manageable changes—perhaps a morning routine adjustment, setting one boundary, or trying a five-minute meditation. Small steps create momentum without overwhelming you.

Allow Time for Healing

Burnout doesn't happen overnight, and recovery won't either. Be patient with yourself and allow the time you need to heal fully. Remember, recovery is a process, and it's okay to take things slowly.

Embrace Growth

Though burnout is challenging, it also brings the opportunity to learn more about yourself. As you work through it, you might discover new strengths, values, or dreams, and change old ones to better serve you. Embrace this as a time of growth and a chance to build resilience for the future.

With that in mind, let's explore several methods that can help restore vitality and reduce stress. Remember, stress is not a bad thing. It is a handy tool which is just out of alignment.

VITALITY

Karen Curry Parker describes burnout as a depletion of our life energy, or vitality. Restoring vitality, she suggests, isn't simply a matter of reducing work hours or switching jobs; it's about reconnecting with core values, purpose, and our inner life force. By addressing deeper causes of burnout, such as unhealed emotional wounds and trauma, people can begin to revive their sense of vitality, leading to more sustainable, fulfilling lives.

Vitality is often defined as the state of being strong, active, and energetic, but it encompasses much more than just physical energy. It includes emotional, mental, and spiritual well-being—the sense of feeling alive, engaged, and connected to our purpose. When we experience prolonged burnout or stress, vitality can be difficult to restore. Understanding the distinction between vitality and resilience can shed some light on why both are crucial in different ways.

While vitality is the zest for life that helps us feel alive and engaged, resilience is the strength that allows us to recover from setbacks. Vitality is about being fully present and enthusiastic, driven by physical energy, mental sharpness, and emotional motivation. Resilience, on the other hand, is our capacity to adapt and bounce back when facing challenges. It involves managing emotions, problem-solving, and drawing on support systems. In essence, vitality enables us to thrive, while resilience helps us endure and recover when life gets tough.

Restoring vitality after burnout requires attention to multiple aspects of life—each step offering a pathway to renewed energy and purpose. Here are some key areas to focus on in your journey toward vitality:

Reconnect with Your Purpose

Rekindling a sense of purpose starts with clarifying what truly matters to you. Take time to identify your core values and set goals that resonate with them. When we align our actions with our values, it becomes easier to tap into our energy and stay motivated. Meaningful goals, rather than those set by external expectations, can restore a sense of direction and purpose.

Nourish Your Body and Mind

Our physical well-being forms the foundation of vitality. Regular exercise, a balanced diet, and sufficient sleep are essential for restoring both physical energy and mental clarity. Mindfulness and meditation can further support well-being by reducing stress, fostering self-awareness, and promoting inner calm, allowing us to approach each day with a more balanced perspective.

Heal Emotional Wounds

Burnout is often linked to unresolved emotional issues or traumas. Working with a therapist or counsellor can help process these underlying wounds, which, in turn, can release emotional energy and improve overall vitality. It's also important to surround yourself with positive, supportive people who help you feel seen and valued, as positive relationships are a significant source of emotional strength.

Manage Stress Effectively

Setting boundaries and learning to say no can be transformative in protecting your energy. Choose to engage only in activities that align with your values and contribute to your well-being. Alongside boundaries, relaxing activities like spending time in nature or pursuing hobbies can help you recharge and unwind from daily pressures.

Engage in Joyful Activities

Taking time to engage in hobbies or interests you're passionate about can significantly boost vitality.

Creative expression, whether through art, music, writing, or any other form, can reconnect you with a sense of aliveness and provide an outlet for emotional release and joy.

Build a Spiritual Connection

For many people, spirituality is a deep source of vitality, offering a sense of connection to something greater than themselves. Whether through prayer, meditation, or time spent in nature, spiritual practices can nurture a feeling of peace and purpose. Practising gratitude can also be powerful, shifting your focus to what's already present and fulfilling in your life.

Live Authentically

One of the most powerful ways to restore vitality is by embracing authenticity. Being true to yourself and living in alignment with your real desires, needs, and values prevents the energy drain that comes from pretending to be someone you're not. By honouring your true self, you conserve and direct your energy toward what genuinely matters to you.

Restoring vitality is a gradual, holistic process that encompasses physical, emotional, mental, and spiritual dimensions. By paying attention to each area, you can revive your energy, enthusiasm, and sense of purpose, empowering you to engage more fully in life once again.

Daily Priming and Visualisation

Tony Robbins developed a concept he calls priming, a form of meditation that helps reshape our belief systems. His priming routine is designed to become a daily ritual, used each morning to manage mindset and set the tone for the day. This process involves several key steps to alter both the state of mind and perception. The video can be found on YouTube under the search "Tony Robbins daily priming".

Physical Activation

Robbins starts with a physical component, which might include focused breathing exercises or brief, invigorating movements to elevate his heart rate. This physical priming prepares the body and mind to engage in the practice more fully.

Gratitude and Visualisation

Priming also involves shifting attention to three things for which he is genuinely grateful, allowing him to connect deeply with these positive feelings. Next, he visualises three goals he wants to achieve, imagining them as already accomplished. This practice fosters a sense of certainty, making these objectives feel attainable and motivating his actions toward them.

Positive Language and Outreach

Robbins emphasises using positive language since the brain processes affirmations more effectively in this form. For example, instead of saying "Don't feel anxious," a statement like "I feel calm and capable" keeps the focus constructive. Robbins also connects with others during priming by sending sincere messages or reaching out to strengthen relationships. This step aligns with Simon Sinek's concept that the brain doesn't interpret negatives effectively, illustrated in his example: "Do not think of a pink elephant"—an instruction that immediately conjures the image of a pink elephant.

Visualisation, when approached thoughtfully, is a powerful mental tool, though it requires caution to avoid slipping into unrealistic thinking. Visualisation can easily cross a line into delusion if not grounded in present reality. Practising visualisation effectively means embracing a balanced approach: creating a mental image of future goals and aspirations while staying rooted in the present.

Eckhart Tolle, particularly in *The Power of Now*, stresses the importance of living in the moment. Tolle believes that anchoring ourselves in the "Now" frees us from future anxieties and past regrets.

Tolle argues that only the present is real, while the past and future exist only in our minds. By living fully in each moment, we align ourselves with life as it unfolds. He advises, "Realise deeply that the present moment is all you ever have."

Much of our suffering, according to Tolle, arises from over-identifying with thoughts tied to the past or future. He encourages us to observe these thoughts without attachment, a practice he calls "witnessing consciousness." This helps us break free from the mind's control, allowing us to live more freely.

Tolle sees the ego as heavily invested in past experiences and future expectations, often causing dissatisfaction. By releasing ourselves from these time-bound thoughts, we achieve a sense of peace, enjoying the simplicity of "being" instead of always "becoming."

Embracing the present requires accepting life as it is rather than resisting it. Tolle's notion of surrender involves aligning with reality, easing inner conflict, and finding peace.

Affirmations alone may fall short if we haven't first accepted reality as it is. Acceptance of our current situation and feelings is essential before shifting toward positive affirmations. This acceptance provides the foundation for focusing on the outcomes we truly want and fostering genuine positive energy.

When we commit to the present, Tolle suggests, we find lasting joy and peace that don't rely on external conditions. This deep state of "presence" connects us with a profound sense of life, extending beyond momentary pleasures.

Stress, Tolle asserts, often results from projecting ourselves into the future, which is ultimately a construct of the imagination. While visualisation can be a tool to paint a picture of the future we want, it's critical to step back afterwards and remain grounded in the present, knowing that we create our future from today's actions.

Visualisation works by mentally rehearsing desired outcomes. When we visualise achieving a goal—like succeeding in a job interview, excelling in a performance, or reaching personal growth milestones—the brain engages many of the same pathways as in the actual experience. This "priming" effect not only prepares us for real-life scenarios but also builds self-confidence. Where attention goes, energy flows.

Visualisation translates abstract dreams into clear intentions, helping us see both the result and the steps required to get there. By mentally rehearsing our goals, we align our actions with our aspirations, creating a focused pathway to success.

Mental rehearsal reduces anxiety by familiarising the brain with potential challenges. Athletes and performers often use this technique to visualise each step of a task, which helps the brain and body respond calmly and confidently when faced with the real thing. Visualisation can also stimulate dopamine release, increasing motivation and encouraging a focused approach. Envisioning success reinforces a positive mindset, fuelling our determination to meet our goals.

Visualisation strengthens self-belief. By repeatedly seeing ourselves succeed, we build confidence and resilience, which enables us to persist through challenges. This mental rehearsal establishes a foundation of self-efficacy essential for achieving long-term goals.

However, delusion—a state where visualisation disconnects from reality—presents a risk. While delusion may offer temporary comfort, it ultimately prevents meaningful progress by diverting energy away from real-world action. Unlike productive visualisation, which is grounded in reality, delusion fosters escapism, leading to avoidance rather than empowerment. When practising visualisation, it's crucial to stay anchored in the present and to address any unresolved trauma. You can't simply say, "I am great!" while continuing to treat others poorly; that's just ego talking. And ego is like a hard, empty tin—rigid on the outside as a defence, but hollow within. Doing the inner work is essential! Visualisation is about creating new brain patterns and beliefs, and to do so effectively, we often need to understand and heal old patterns first.

Delusion often stems from unresolved fears and magical thinking, while true visualisation arises from accepting the present and imagining a better future with intention.

The human ego is essentially our sense of self, our identity, and our perception of "who we are." It's the voice in our minds that helps us distinguish ourselves from others, creating a mental boundary that separates "me" from "you" or "us" from "them." This sense of self is built up through our beliefs, memories, experiences, and the roles we play in life, and it strongly shapes our thoughts, emotions, and behaviours.

While the ego can be a source of strength, ambition, and motivation, it can also lead to challenges. The ego often operates to protect us, serving as a kind of mental armour against perceived threats to our self-image or identity. When someone criticises or challenges us, the ego might react defensively, as if it's protecting something fragile and essential. This protective nature can be useful for self-preservation, but it can also make us resistant to change or constructive feedback.

The ego frequently pushes us to seek external validation, success, and approval. It's often concerned with how we're perceived by others, which can drive us toward accomplishments, status, and material possessions. While this can motivate us to achieve our goals, it can also lead to dissatisfaction if we become overly attached to these things as sources of happiness. The ego tends to measure itself against others, creating a sense of competition and hierarchy. It's why we might feel envious, superior, or inferior depending on our comparisons with others. This trait of the ego can lead to feelings of insecurity, resentment, or even arrogance if left unchecked.

The ego doesn't typically embrace vulnerability, as it can be seen as a weakness. Instead, it prefers to project strength, control, and certainty, often masking deeper fears, insecurities, or unresolved issues. This resistance can make it difficult for people to open up, ask for help, or admit mistakes.

Many spiritual traditions, including those taught by Eckhart Tolle, Carl Jung, and others, suggest that the ego is only a limited aspect of who we truly are. According to this view, beneath the ego lies the "true self" or a deeper, more authentic sense of being that isn't defined by external identities, accomplishments, or validations. Practices like mindfulness, meditation, and self-reflection can help individuals "step back" from the ego, allowing them to observe it without becoming overly attached to it.

In a healthy sense, the ego can help us set boundaries, develop resilience, and pursue our passions. However, when the ego is overly dominant or defensive, it can lead to negative behaviours, such as self-centeredness, rigidity, and conflict with others. Recognising and understanding the ego—without letting it take control—is a valuable part of personal growth. It's about balancing the ego's needs with empathy, awareness, and a connection to a deeper, more meaningful sense of self. Visualisation works more effectively when the ego is in check.

In summary, visualisation is a potent mental tool that helps us rehearse for success, boost confidence, maintain focus on our aspirations and replace old patterns with new ones. However, to be genuinely constructive, it must remain rooted in reality. Without this grounding, visualisation can easily become delusional, trapping us in fantasies that hinder true growth and forward momentum.

LETTING GO OF EMOTIONS

Dealing with emotions and past traumas is a crucial part of life that is often overlooked. Many of us don't fully understand the role emotions play, leading to patterns of suppression or explosive outbursts.

Gabor Maté, a renowned physician and author, emphasises the powerful role emotions play in our health and well-being. He explains that emotions are not just fleeting psychological states; they are deeply intertwined with our physical health and sense of self. According to Maté, how we handle emotions—whether we suppress them, ignore them, or express them impulsively—has a profound impact on our overall health.

Maté asserts that emotions are essential signals. They alert us to what is happening within and around us, indicating when something requires attention, whether it's a boundary that needs setting or an emotion that needs exploring. Processing and expressing emotions in a healthy way enables us to protect our needs, communicate authentically, and form meaningful connections. However, suppressing emotions, Maté warns, can lead to "emotional dis-ease," which may manifest as mental health struggles, chronic illness, and a diminished sense of personal authenticity.

Maté observes that many people habitually ignore or suppress difficult emotions like anger, sadness, or grief, often due to societal expectations or learned behaviours from early family dynamics. In his clinical work, he notes that suppressing emotions over time can contribute to health issues, from autoimmune diseases to depression. When ignored, difficult emotions don't disappear; instead, they become stored in the body, with this residual emotional energy frequently resurfacing as physical symptoms. The body, as Maté often suggests, "remembers" emotions that the mind consciously ignores.

Suppression of emotions, especially beginning in childhood, can lead to unhealthy coping mechanisms, such as addiction or dysfunctional relationships in adulthood. Children discouraged from expressing certain emotions often learn to detach from these feelings entirely, associating emotions with discomfort or rejection. As adults, this detachment can contribute to substance abuse, unfulfilling relationships, and a weakened sense of self, with emotions operating subconsciously, influencing decisions and creating emotional blocks.

While Maté stresses the importance of expressing emotions, he also makes a distinction between constructive release and impulsive expression. Exploding in anger or letting emotions erupt uncontrollably is not the solution he advocates. While such outbursts might feel like a "release," they are often a result of pent-up suppression. The healthy approach is to observe, understand, and release emotions in ways that neither harm us nor others.

For processing emotions in a way that promotes both mental and physical well-being, Maté encourages "compassionate inquiry." This process involves observing and understanding emotions without judgment or resistance. It means being mindfully aware of emotions as they arise, accepting and acknowledging them rather than attempting to change or fix them immediately, and exploring their origins with curiosity. Taking the time to ask ourselves why a certain emotion has surfaced and allowing ourselves to sit with it reveals valuable insights into our inner lives. Healthy outlets, such as journaling, sharing with trusted friends, or engaging in creative pursuits, can further support the release and integration of emotions, transforming what might feel overwhelming into greater self-understanding.

Authenticity—aligning our actions and self-expression with our true feelings—is essential for both emotional and physical health. Living authentically does not mean adopting "positive thinking" or forcing happiness; it's about being true to our inner experiences, even when they're challenging. Suppressing emotions to fit in or appear "strong" disconnects us from our true selves, often leaving us feeling isolated, anxious, and unfulfilled.

Cultivating a healthy relationship with emotions involves neither repression nor unchecked expression. Instead, it requires a mindful, compassionate approach that allows us to experience emotions fully and release them constructively. By honouring the messages each emotion brings, we foster both physical health and emotional resilience, underscoring the deep connection between the mind, body, and spirit. Embracing emotional authenticity can be a powerful act of healing and self-compassion.

David Hawkins, in *Letting Go: The Pathway of Surrender*, offers a three-step approach to handling emotions through what he calls the "method of surrender." This process helps individuals experience emotions fully without letting them take control.

Acknowledge the Feeling: Instead of resisting or intellectualising emotions, Hawkins advises simply allowing the feeling to exist, accepting it without judgment. This first step creates a space where emotions can be observed rather than suppressed or fought.

Stay with the Feeling: After acknowledging the emotion, Hawkins suggests staying present with it, allowing the sensation to unfold. This involves resisting the urge to escape or act impulsively, giving the emotion room to rise and naturally subside.

Release the Emotion: Finally, Hawkins emphasises letting the emotion dissipate on its own without holding onto it or analysing it further. This release happens naturally as we detach from the feeling, leading to inner peace and emotional clarity.

Hawkins' method of surrender promotes balance and freedom from emotional entanglement, allowing emotions to move through us rather than define or overwhelm us.

Redirecting your life is about changing how you think, accepting things as they are, acknowledging past traumas, and focusing on what you want rather than what you wish to avoid. Resisting keeps feeding the issue (where attention goes, energy flows!).

Change begins with acceptance, which allows us to refocus on what we want.

Look for any potential positives or opportunities in a situation. Once the weight of unresolved issues is lifted, redirect attention toward fulfilling what you want or enjoy.

Another technique, sometimes called "stone piling," suggests treating emotions like the tantrums of a three-year-old. Just as with a child's outburst, acknowledge the emotion, pick it up momentarily, comfort it, and set it back down. By symbolically "piling" these emotions, we allow ourselves to feel and then release them.

Affirmations or mantras can be powerful tools for personal growth, but their effectiveness relies on thoughtful application. They work by replacing negative thought patterns with constructive, optimistic beliefs. Regularly practising affirmations can train the mind to focus on positive outcomes, fostering self-empowerment and boosting self-esteem. They can also aid in mindfulness by prompting individuals to centre on positive statements, helping to improve emotional regulation and resilience.

Affirmations are most effective when coupled with realistic goals and actions. Repeating affirmations without action can lead to disappointment, so it's essential that affirmations are rooted in genuine self-belief rather than becoming empty words. Although research on affirmations varies, studies show they can reduce stress and enhance performance, largely depending on the individual's mindset and belief in their affirmations.

FOCUS TIME

In this section, focus time refers to making one's daily tasks more productive — managing the workload more efficiently by setting aside "focus time" at the optimal time of day.

Dr Mithu Storoni and Andrew Huberman emphasise the importance of optimising focus time for better productivity and cognitive performance. They suggest that the human brain functions best in concentrated bursts of around 25 to 45 minutes, allowing for heightened focus and efficiency. Some individuals may extend these focused sessions to 60–90 minutes, but beyond that, maintaining peak concentration becomes difficult. Once a focus session concludes, Storoni and Huberman advise shifting to tasks that require less concentration, allowing for a flexible approach to work.

To harness this focused time effectively, both experts recommend techniques like the Pomodoro Technique, which involves working in short, intense intervals followed by short breaks. These breaks give the brain a chance to recharge, preventing mental fatigue and enabling sustained attention. Huberman highlights the role of neurotransmitters—particularly dopamine—in motivation and focus, noting that managing dopamine levels can enhance our ability to concentrate.

Storoni also stresses the importance of creating an optimal focus environment by minimising distractions and setting clear goals for each session. Together, their insights illustrate that managing focus time with well-timed breaks can boost productivity and support cognitive health, while also helping to reduce stress and improve resilience.

Structured focus sessions break tasks into manageable intervals, helping to prevent the overwhelm that can come from tackling large, complex projects all at once. Focusing on specific, short-term goals encourages a sense of achievement, boosting motivation and decreasing the likelihood of procrastination. Short breaks between these sessions play a vital role in mental recovery, allowing individuals to step away, recharge, and clear their minds—which is the key to reducing fatigue and anxiety.

By fostering small wins, focus sessions help individuals feel more in control of their workload, promoting a sense of accomplishment that can lead to higher job satisfaction and a healthier work environment. Additionally, the structure of focused intervals supports better routines, improving self-awareness of mental states and encouraging timely breaks to prevent stress from escalating into burnout.

High cortisol levels, often linked to burnout, heighten reactivity and diminish creativity. When cortisol is elevated, the body's "fight or flight" response kicks in, physiologically limiting access to the brain's creative centres. In contrast, maintaining vitality and avoiding burnout allows for a more expansive mental state, supporting creativity and innovation. By respecting the body's natural rhythm of focus and rest, individuals can mitigate stress, manage cortisol levels, and access a clearer, more creative mind.

Yoga Nidra

Yoga Nidra, or "yogic sleep," is a practice of deep, conscious relaxation that allows the mind and body to rest while remaining alert. Often referred to as "effortless relaxation," this state of awareness is achieved by lying down comfortably and guiding the body into a state of profound restfulness without drifting into unconscious sleep.

In Yoga Nidra, practitioners hover between wakefulness and sleep, where the body reaches a natural balance, or homeostasis, and the breath becomes calm and steady. This balanced state opens the flow of prana, or life energy, within the body, promoting relaxation that often surpasses other meditation practices. By dissolving blockages to prana's flow, Yoga Nidra helps ease stress, improve overall health, and calm the nervous system. For many, it is a therapeutic tool for addressing chronic stress, trauma, and conditions like PTSD.

I've personally found Yoga Nidra incredibly helpful for recharging during a busy day and for getting deeper rest at night. A quick 15-minute script works wonders on stressful days, while at bedtime, I often choose a one-hour session to promote a more restful sleep. There are plenty of guided scripts on YouTube, making it easy to find the right length and style for any need.

Yoga Nidra affects two key components of memory: absorbing new information and recalling it. In this practice, the mind becomes deeply receptive, allowing information to settle into the subconscious while maintaining an elevated state of awareness. Practising Yoga Nidra regularly can also enhance sleep quality by teaching the body and mind to relax, letting go of stress and making it easier to transition into deep sleep at bedtime.

This profound relaxation reduces stress, anxiety, and physical tension, often bringing a sense of inner calm and rejuvenation. Through guided sessions that include body and breath awareness, as well as visualisation techniques, Yoga Nidra can facilitate emotional healing, increase creativity, and support both mental and physical health. It has shown benefits in managing pain, reducing insomnia, and fostering a deep-seated sense of peace. The accessibility of this practice—suitable for people of all ages and physical abilities—makes it an appealing choice for those seeking rest without intense physical effort.

While Yoga Nidra and meditation share some similarities, they are distinct practices. In meditation, one is typically seated and consciously focusing, letting thoughts flow in and out while remaining in a waking state. Meditation often brings practitioners into a theta brainwave state, which is the gateway to the deep, delta state of healing sleep.

In contrast, Yoga Nidra is a journey through different states of consciousness, where one moves from wakefulness into dreaming and beyond, reaching a state of "conscious sleep." In this state, practitioners can enter the delta brainwave state while still maintaining awareness, a condition that offers the body and mind the opportunity to rest and heal deeply.

Yoga Nidra is also a valuable tool in yogic philosophy for working with samskaras (mental impressions, psychological imprints, or habitual patterns formed by past experiences, actions, and thoughts, which are stored in the subconscious). Samskaras shape our responses and behaviours, often subconsciously, influencing how we react to present situations. By addressing these patterns in a relaxed and receptive state, Yoga Nidra can help individuals recognise and release negative habits, foster positive changes, and support self-awareness and personal growth.

Although Yoga Nidra brings deep relaxation, it does not replace regular, rejuvenating sleep, which typically requires 7–9 hours. During the day, however, Yoga Nidra can act as a restorative "charge," much like a short walk or a mindful break, providing an energy boost without sleep. Regular practice offers both physical and mental renewal, making it a powerful tool for maintaining balance and wellness in daily life.

Meditation

Meditation has long been a powerful tool for combating stress and burnout, as it promotes relaxation, reduces cortisol, and cultivates a calm, focused mindset. By centring attention on the breath or a chosen point of focus, meditation eases the body out of its fight-or-flight mode, calming the nervous system. This relaxation response helps us manage our stress triggers more effectively, enhancing emotional regulation and creating resilience against burnout. Over time, regular meditation practice leads to greater self-awareness, enabling a more balanced, less reactive response to daily challenges.

Meditation offers a range of approaches, making it adaptable to different needs, whether for relaxation, anxiety relief, or even to improve health outcomes, such as easing the process of quitting smoking. It's an ancient practice, spanning thousands of years and cultures, yet scientific research on meditation is relatively new. Modern technology has enabled a deeper understanding of meditation's effects on the brain and body, revealing how it improves mental well-being and resilience.

There's no single correct way to meditate; meditation comes in various forms, each with its unique benefits. Here are some of the most common types:

Body-Centred Meditation: Also known as self-scanning, this type involves focusing on physical sensations throughout the body, allowing a deeper connection with bodily awareness.

Contemplation: This involves concentrating on a question or paradox without letting the mind wander, promoting mental focus and clarity.

Emotion-Centred Meditation: This form encourages focusing on a specific emotion, such as kindness or gratitude, which can enhance positive emotional experiences.

Mantra Meditation: In this form, a specific phrase or sound is repeated either aloud or silently, helping the mind find stillness and clarity.

Meditation with Movement: This includes focusing on the breath while moving or even walking with full awareness of surroundings. Practices like Tai Chi and certain forms of yoga incorporate this meditative movement.

Mindfulness Meditation: Focused on the present moment, mindfulness meditation encourages awareness of sensations, thoughts, or feelings without judgment. Often grounded in body-centred awareness, it's one of the most popular forms today.

Visual-Based Meditation: In this type, attention is placed on a physical object or a mental image, which can serve as an anchor for concentration and calm.

Meditation is a flexible practice, accessible to everyone, and can be customised to fit various lifestyles and needs. By developing mindfulness and self-awareness through meditation, individuals not only manage stress but also foster a sense of inner calm and resilience, qualities essential for thriving in a fast-paced world.

exercise

Exercise is a powerful antidote to burnout and stress, with the potential to elevate mood, reduce cortisol levels, and enhance overall well-being. Incorporating heart rate-boosting activities into your routine offers a natural way to enhance well-being, especially during burnout recovery. Exercise increases dopamine release in the body, often called the "feel-good" neurotransmitter, which contributes to improved mood, mental clarity, and stress relief. Activities like aerobic exercise — jogging, cycling, or even brisk walking — support cardiovascular health while helping manage stress and build resilience. Mind-body exercises, such as yoga and tai chi, go a step further by combining physical movement with breathwork, helping to calm the nervous system and foster mindfulness. Strength training can also aid in this process, enhancing not just physical strength but mental resilience and confidence as well.

Making a variety of enjoyable activities part of your routine is essential to make exercise sustainable. Even just 10-30 minutes daily can improve mood, boost energy, and provide a valuable outlet for relieving stress. Exercise also enhances sleep quality by helping to reduce fatigue and promote a calm state conducive to better rest. Additionally, regular movement supports cognitive function, stimulating blood flow and encouraging brain cell growth, which can improve memory and thinking skills.

Yoga is highly effective in managing stress by calming the nervous system and reducing cortisol, a key stress hormone. With its deep breathing and controlled movement, yoga promotes mindfulness and a stronger mind-body connection. Practised regularly, it builds resilience against stress and improves sleep quality, often cultivating a supportive sense of community in group classes.

In *The Body Keeps the Score* by Dr Bessel van der Kolk explores how yoga can be an effective tool for healing trauma and rebuilding the connection between mind and body, which trauma often disrupts. He describes how survivors of trauma frequently struggle with feeling detached or numb, as traumatic experiences can leave them disconnected from their own physical sensations. Yoga, however, offers a pathway for individuals to reconnect safely with their bodies. Through slow, mindful movements and breath control, yoga encourages an awareness of bodily sensations, allowing trauma survivors to start observing and accepting feelings that might have been suppressed or ignored.

Van der Kolk highlights yoga's role in regulating the nervous system, which is often thrown off balance by trauma. People who have experienced trauma may find their fight-or-flight response activated frequently, even in safe environments, which makes it challenging to feel calm or relaxed. Yoga can help to counteract this by engaging the parasympathetic nervous system, also known as the "rest and digest" response. By focusing on breath and relaxation techniques, yoga practitioners can achieve a state of calm that brings the nervous system back into balance, helping to cultivate a sense of safety and relaxation.

Another benefit of yoga, according to van der Kolk, is its ability to help release physical tension stored in the body. Trauma often leaves its mark in the form of muscle tightness or chronic pain, which yoga can gently alleviate through stretching and movement. As the body lets go of this physical "armour," survivors may find that they are also able to release some of the emotional weight associated with their trauma, allowing for a more holistic form of healing.

For trauma survivors, yoga can be empowering in ways that other forms of therapy may not be. Trauma often involves a loss of control, and through yoga, individuals are given the opportunity to make choices about their own movements, fostering a sense of autonomy and self-trust. In a safe, judgment-free space, survivors can begin to reclaim agency over their bodies, which can be deeply affirming and therapeutic.

Finally, van der Kolk discusses the power of mindfulness in yoga to bring individuals back to the present moment. Trauma survivors often feel trapped in the past, haunted by intrusive memories and anxieties. Yoga, with its emphasis on the here and now, helps practitioners to focus on their breath, their posture, and their movements, which quiets the mind and provides relief from past worries. For many, this practice of presence becomes a refuge, a place where they can experience calm, resilience, and a renewed sense of connection with themselves.

Van der Kolk's work ultimately positions yoga as a valuable, complementary practice for those recovering from trauma, one that supports traditional therapeutic approaches by reconnecting mind and body, regulating emotions, and building resilience in a compassionate and structured way.

Talk Therapy

Talk therapy is a highly effective tool for managing stress and burnout, offering a secure space to process complex emotions, identify stressors, and develop lasting coping strategies. Approaches like cognitive-behavioural therapy (CBT) and mindfulness-based stress reduction (MBSR) are particularly beneficial, helping to reframe negative thought patterns, cultivate relaxation techniques, and increase self-awareness. Therapy promotes emotional resilience, allowing individuals to address core issues such as self-worth, boundary-setting, and unresolved trauma. In doing so, it provides a sustainable path for stress management and personal growth, helping to prevent future episodes of burnout.

Engaging in talk therapy with a licensed professional—be it a psychologist, psychiatric nurse, counsellor, social worker, or psychiatrist—offers an environment to explore not only external stressors, such as work demands, but also internal reactions. This process fosters self-awareness, helping individuals recognise personal needs and make empowered choices to regain control over their lives. During initial sessions, the therapist might identify the most appropriate approach, such as CBT or behavioural therapy, based on an individual's specific needs and goals. Therapy also builds a support network beyond the workplace, provides a foundation for addressing related mental health challenges like anxiety or depression, and strengthens relationships with family, colleagues, and others. Notably, talk therapy is effective as a non-medicated approach, with research from the American Psychological Association suggesting that around 75 percent of participants experience meaningful improvement through therapeutic work.

In some cases, a therapist or doctor may recommend antidepressants as part of the treatment plan. While medication can offer relief, it's essential to weigh the pros and cons with a healthcare provider. Alternatively, natural supplements are available at most pharmacies, which may help increase serotonin levels. However, these options should also be discussed with a healthcare provider to ensure they align with any other health considerations.

The therapy process typically starts with an initial session where the therapist gathers essential information, including background, mental health history, past traumas, coping mechanisms, and therapeutic goals. This understanding allows the therapist to create a tailored treatment plan. Talk therapy then unfolds as an open-ended dialogue, providing space to discuss family life, relationships, childhood experiences, and any symptoms related to burnout or mental health. Session frequency varies based on personal needs—some people attend regularly until they've achieved a solid foundation for lifestyle improvements, deeper self-understanding, and personal growth. Building rapport with a therapist is crucial, and if the connection feels lacking, it's okay to seek out another professional who feels like a better fit.

Walk-and-talk therapy has also emerged as a promising approach, combining the benefits of traditional therapy with the calming and reflective qualities of the outdoors. Research highlights that sessions conducted in nature, particularly during seasons with more sunlight and greenery, can enhance the therapeutic experience and deepen the sense of restoration. Dr Tara Swart explains how trees such as pine, fir, palms, cedar, and cypress release phytoncides, compounds that interact with the immune system to help fight off harmful cells. Simply being in a natural environment, viewing it, or walking through it can support mental health and create a more impactful therapeutic experience.

Burnout can feel overwhelming, affecting one's physical, emotional, and mental well-being. Often, a first response is to withdraw, seeking respite in solitude. The descent into burnout can happen quickly, yet recovery is a gradual journey. Therapy helps individuals find a path back, offering support and insights to foster resilience, patience, and sustained healing.

Healthy Diet

A healthy diet plays a crucial role in managing stress and aiding recovery from burnout by positively impacting energy levels, mood, and resilience. Nutrient-dense foods such as leafy greens, whole grains, nuts, and legumes help regulate blood sugar, sustain brain health, and provide consistent energy throughout the day, which enhances focus and emotional stability. Including sources of omega-3 fatty acids—like fish, flaxseeds, and walnuts—supports brain function and reduces inflammation, helping to alleviate stress-related symptoms.

Limiting caffeine, sugar, and processed foods is also key, as these can cause energy spikes and crashes, increase irritability, and worsen anxiety. Magnesium-rich foods, like leafy greens and bananas, help calm the nervous system, while foods high in vitamin C, such as citrus fruits, reduce cortisol, the primary stress hormone. Embracing these dietary habits can lead to improved mood stability, heightened resilience, and a smoother, more sustained recovery from burnout.

Another thing to consider and you would need to see which health care providers in your area provide the service, is DNA testing. DNA testing can offer valuable insights into how our unique genetic makeup influences our health, dietary needs, and even stress response. By analysing specific genetic markers, DNA tests can reveal predispositions to certain nutrient deficiencies, metabolic tendencies, and how our bodies process various foods. This information allows for personalised dietary adjustments, which can help optimise energy levels, improve digestion, and support mental health. For stress management, DNA testing can uncover genetic markers related to neurotransmitter production, stress hormone regulation, and even sleep quality, helping individuals understand why they may be more prone to anxiety, fatigue, or poor sleep under stress. With these insights, people can make targeted lifestyle changes to boost resilience, balance mood, and enhance overall well-being, creating a proactive approach to health that aligns with their biology.

Breathwork

Breathwork is an incredibly powerful tool for managing stress and burnout, as it directly affects the body's physiological responses and can quickly shift the mind's state. By consciously controlling your breath, you can activate the parasympathetic nervous system, which promotes relaxation and counteracts the fight-or-flight response triggered by stress. Simple breathing techniques, such as deep diaphragmatic breathing, box breathing, and alternate nostril breathing, are all effective methods for calming the mind, reducing cortisol levels, lowering heart rate, and increasing oxygen flow to the brain, which helps enhance clarity and focus. Deep diaphragmatic breathing, or belly breathing, is particularly helpful for reducing stress by slowing the heart rate and promoting a sense of calm. Box breathing, where you inhale, hold, exhale, and hold again for a count of four, helps reset your focus and improve emotional regulation in stressful moments. Alternate nostril breathing, believed to balance the body's energy, enhances concentration and emotional stability, especially beneficial during periods of burnout.

Andrew Huberman, frequently emphasises the power of breath in controlling heart rate. He suggests that making your exhales longer and more vigorous than your inhales can significantly slow your heart rate and promote relaxation. By incorporating these breathwork techniques into your daily routine, you can reduce stress, stay grounded in the present moment, and break the cycle of anxiety that often accompanies burnout.

Breathing practices not only help manage stress but also support a broader mindset of relaxation and surrender. Slowing down, both physically and mentally, allows life to flow more smoothly, and it opens the door for your inner brilliance to shine. In moments of stress, remember that what you focus on grows, and by shifting your attention to calming breathwork, you can redirect your energy from burnout to a state of flow. Embracing practices like mindfulness, gratitude, and self-care, which are essential to wholehearted living, can protect your mental and emotional health and help cultivate resilience, authenticity, and self-compassion. This holistic approach significantly reduces the risk of burnout by fostering balance and connection in both personal and professional life. In times of difficulty, building willpower through challenging tasks can strengthen your mental toughness and resilience. Though it may be hard to start, pushing through resistance, especially when doing something meaningful, fuels passion and enhances your overall well-being.

In the book *Breathe In, Breathe Out*, Stuart Sandeman highlights how breathwork can be a transformative tool for managing stress, enhancing mental clarity, and improving emotional well-being. The book shares practical breathing exercises to help reduce stress, with some key techniques that are particularly useful in high-pressure situations. A highly recommended read and he provides several practical breathing techniques.

One effective practice discussed is "infinity breathing," where you inhale and exhale without pausing in between, helping to calm the nervous system and release anxiety. Sandeman also describes exercises that improve focus, such as alternate nostril breathing, which is designed to balance the body and mind. For pain management and emotional release, he suggests visualisations like imagining a nurturing light carrying away discomfort.

The key takeaway from the book is that breathwork can serve as a simple yet powerful tool to reset your emotional state, manage stress, and foster a deeper connection to your mind and body. With over 40 different exercises provided, Sandeman offers a variety of ways to incorporate breathwork into daily life, all aimed at restoring health and mental clarity.

Anhedonia

When burnout goes untreated, it can lead to severe physical, emotional, and mental health consequences. Chronic stress from burnout increases the risk of conditions like heart disease, high blood pressure, and a weakened immune system. Over time, the toll on the body becomes harder to ignore, leading to more serious health issues. Mentally, untreated burnout can manifest as persistent anxiety, depression, and a sense of hopelessness. These feelings often erode self-esteem and motivation, making it difficult to keep up with daily tasks or responsibilities. In professional settings, burnout can result in reduced productivity, higher absenteeism, and greater job turnover. Socially, it can isolate individuals, creating a rift in relationships and fostering feelings of loneliness. Ignoring burnout can ultimately affect nearly every aspect of a person's life, making early recognition and intervention crucial.

One of the lesser-known but significant symptoms of untreated burnout is anhedonia, which is the inability to experience pleasure from activities that are typically enjoyable, such as eating, socialising, or pursuing hobbies. Anhedonia is a core symptom of mental health conditions, particularly depression and schizophrenia, but it can also be linked to anxiety, PTSD, and substance use disorders. When we are overwhelmed by stress, the brain's reward system becomes less responsive, making it harder to derive joy from previously pleasurable experiences.

    Burnout can be a significant trigger for anhedonia. Anhedonia often stems from prolonged stress, particularly when it overwhelms the brain's reward system. As stress persists, it can lead to changes in brain chemistry, especially in areas such as the prefrontal cortex and basal ganglia, which control motivation and pleasure. Chronic exposure to stress not only affects physical health but can also trigger emotional numbness, making it difficult to enjoy even the simplest pleasures. This lack of joy can be compounded by underlying mental health conditions like depression or anxiety, which are commonly associated with anhedonia. Additionally, trauma—especially emotional or physical trauma—can further deepen the disconnect from previously enjoyable activities, especially for those with post-traumatic stress disorder (PTSD). Furthermore, substance abuse or certain medications, such as antidepressants or antipsychotics, may alter brain function, exacerbating the emotional numbness that characterises anhedonia.

    Fortunately, anhedonia can be treated, though recovery requires a multifaceted approach. Cognitive Behavioural Therapy (CBT) is an effective tool for addressing the negative thought patterns that contribute to the condition. Medications like antidepressants (SSRIs or SNRIs) can also help, although responses vary. For those with anhedonia linked to dopamine dysfunction, dopamine-enhancing medications may provide relief. Alongside therapy and medication, lifestyle changes such as regular exercise, mindfulness practices, and social support play crucial roles in recovery. Exercise stimulates the brain's reward system, while mindfulness and meditation promote emotional regulation. Reconnecting with friends and family can help reintroduce social joy, counteracting the isolation that often accompanies anhedonia. Although finding the right treatment combination may take time, it is possible to overcome anhedonia, restoring the ability to experience pleasure and meaning in life once again.

80

Who is more prone to burnout?

"Burnout, unfairly, is most likely to be experienced by good people," Dr Gordon Parker remarks, shedding light on a crucial insight into who tends to be more vulnerable to burnout. The individuals most prone to burnout are often those who are perfectionists, workaholics, people-pleasers, and highly sensitive, deeply caring individuals. These are the people who are dedicated, responsible, and often go above and beyond for their work or those they care for—traits that, when left unchecked, can set the stage for burnout.

Dr Parker explains that these individuals bring with them predisposing behavioural factors—such as high levels of responsibility, reliability, and conscientiousness—which make them more susceptible to stress. This vulnerability, when combined with a stressful event or a series of stressful situations, can trigger a burnout episode. He likens this to other conditions, like schizophrenia or bipolar disorder, where certain people are more prone to experiencing significant mental health challenges due to their personality traits.

Perfectionists are at high risk of burnout because they often display symptoms such as anxiety, depression, irritability, sleep disturbances, and a lack of motivation or passion—symptoms that overlap with those of burnout. These individuals work tirelessly, refusing to take breaks or admit to flaws, driven by the belief that they must meet impossibly high standards. This constant pursuit of perfection sets up a cycle of stress, anxiety, and self-criticism that can eventually lead to burnout.

While perfectionism can seem like an intractable trait, Dr Parker highlights that it is possible to change. Perfectionists often catastrophise, viewing any mistake as a disaster, which leads to anxiety and paralysis, and procrastination sets in as they fear making errors. This behaviour is closely linked to burnout, as perfectionists struggle to find satisfaction in their achievements, focusing instead on any minor flaws. However, cognitive restructuring—learning to accept mistakes and set realistic goals—can help perfectionists reduce their stress and manage burnout more effectively. Embracing imperfection and recognising that mistakes are a natural part of growth can help them find balance and fulfilment without the crushing weight of unrealistic expectations.

Similarly, workaholics face a heightened risk of burnout. Their work is often their primary source of self-worth, and they tend to neglect self-care in favour of productivity. The cycle of overworking is difficult to break, especially for those who come from a performance-oriented background where achievement is prioritised. To avoid burnout, workaholics are encouraged to develop emotional intelligence, track their time to identify areas of unproductive busyness, and seek support from others to balance work with relaxation and fun.

People-pleasers are also at risk, as their desire to make others happy often leads them to overcommit, sacrificing their own needs. This lack of boundary-setting can lead to emotional exhaustion. To combat this, people-pleasers should focus on assertive communication, learning to say no when necessary, and prioritising self-reflection to better understand their limits and needs.

Finally, highly sensitive individuals, who are attuned to the emotions of others and often take on emotional burdens, are also vulnerable to burnout. Their empathy and emotional resilience can lead them to suppress their own feelings to maintain strength for others. This emotional suppression can accumulate over time, contributing to burnout. Sensitive individuals are encouraged to practice grounding techniques and mindfulness to manage sensory overload and maintain emotional balance.

Moreover, certain personality traits, such as high neuroticism and low agreeableness, can make people more prone to burnout. Those with high neuroticism are more likely to experience negative emotions, which increases their susceptibility to work-related stress. On the other hand, individuals with high levels of extraversion, openness, and agreeableness tend to be more resilient and better able to seek social support, helping to protect against burnout.

Recognising these traits and tendencies in oneself or others is a crucial first step in preventing burnout. By acknowledging the factors that make certain individuals more vulnerable, such as perfectionism, workaholism, people-pleasing tendencies, and high sensitivity, proactive measures can be taken to manage stress. Setting boundaries, practising self-care, and fostering emotional resilience are key strategies in this process, allowing individuals to find a sustainable balance between their personal and professional lives while avoiding the physical, emotional, and mental exhaustion of burnout.

Aspiration is working hard for something we hate, and it creates stress. Working hard for something we love is passion.

The future is not real, it is a fiction of our imagination. The present is real. Living in the future creates stress.

About the Author

Monya Maxwell is a photographer, writer, and resilient single mom whose life has been a tapestry of creativity, challenges, and comebacks. With over nine years of professional photography experience and a background in project management, Monya brings a unique perspective to balancing career, motherhood, and personal growth.

Passionate about storytelling, Monya uses her creative outlets—photography and writing—to inspire others. Her work focuses on empowerment, resilience, and finding light in the darkest moments. She is the author of the Shits and Giggles series, which dives into life's unspoken dilemmas with honesty, wit, and a touch of irreverence.

In her latest book, Shits and Giggles - Screw Burnout!, Monya shares hard-won insights on overcoming burnout, reclaiming your spark, and embracing the messy, beautiful journey of life. When she's not writing or photographing stories of endurance, Monya volunteers for a local charity supporting the homeless and cherishes time with her children.

Connect with Monya and explore her creative work at www.monya.co.za.

Reference list

Advancing States. (n.d.). Caregiving in a diverse America. https://www.advancingstates.org/hcbs/article/caregiving-diverse-america

American Psychological Association. (2011, March). Finding your calling. GradPsych. https://www.apa.org/gradpsych/2011/03/corner

Brown, B. (2022). The gifts of imperfection: Let go of who you think you're supposed to be and embrace who you are. Simon and Schuster.

Cleveland Clinic. (n.d.). Meditation: What it is, benefits & types. Cleveland Clinic. Retrieved October 30, 2024, from https://my.clevelandclinic.org/health/articles/17906-meditation

Cohen, L. (2023, January 19). How perfectionism leads to burnout—and what you can do about it. TIME. https://time.com/6244829/burnout-mental-health-perfectionism/

Curry Parker, K. (2023, March 10). A better job won't help - The truth about burnout [Video]. TEDxColoradoSprings. YouTube. https://www.youtube.com/watch?v=G-294NywwZ4

Farber, B. A. (2000). Treatment strategies for different types of teacher burnout. Journal of Clinical psychology, 56(5), 675-689.

Frankl, V. E. (2006). Man's search for meaning (I. Lasch, Trans.). Beacon Press. (Original work published 1946)

Freudenberger, H. J. (1974). Staff burn-out. Journal of social issues, 30(1), 159-165.

Goggins, D., & Huberman, A. (2023, January 5). How to build willpower [Video]. YouTube. https://www.youtube.com/watch?v=84dYijIpWjQ

Hawkins, D. R. (2012). Letting go: The pathway of surrender. Hay House.

Howes, L. (2023, July 24). Are you lazy or just burned out? (Tips to overcome both) [Video]. YouTube. https://www.youtube.com/watch?v=OA_84PQ8fbo

Rosenthal, E. (2023, October 18). Six ways to deal with parental burnout. Greater Good Science Center at UC Berkeley. https://greatergood.berkeley.edu/article/item/six_ways_to_deal_with_parental_burnout

Roloff, J., Kirstges, J., Grund, S., & Klusmann, U. (2022). How strongly is personality associated with burnout among teachers? A meta-analysis. Educational Psychology Review, 34, 1613–1650. https://doi.org/10.1007/s10648-022-09672-7

Snowden, R. (2005). Jung: The key ideas. Hodder & Stoughton.

Tomaszek, K., & Muchacka-Cymerman, A. (2022). Student burnout and PTSD symptoms: The role of existential anxiety and academic fears on students during the COVID 19 pandemic. Depression research and treatment, 2022(1), 6979310.

van den Berg, A. E., & Beute, F. (2021). Walk it off! The effectiveness of walk and talk coaching in nature for individuals with burnout-and stress-related complaints. Journal of Environmental Psychology, 76, 101641.

WHO: Burn-out an "occupational phenomenon": International Classification of Diseases. https://www.who.int/news/item/28-05-2019-burn-out-an-occupational-phenomenon-international-classification-of-diseases

YogaUOnline. (n.d.). 7 amazing benefits of Yoga Nidra. YogaUOnline. Retrieved October 30, 2024, from https://yogauonline.com/yoga-health-benefits/yoga-for-stress-relief/7-amazing-benefits-of-yoga-nidra/

We are meant to grow,

so we have something to give.

Find out more about Monya –

www.monya.co.za

Shits and Giggles – Diaries of a Solo Mom

In Shits and Giggles - Diaries of a Solo Mom, Monya Maxwell fearlessly dives into the raw, unfiltered realities of single motherhood, shattering stereotypes and stigmas along the way. With candid storytelling and a dash of humour, she shares her journey of resilience, offering empowering insights and practical wisdom for single mothers everywhere. This book is a testament to the strength, courage, and unwavering love that define single mothers as they navigate the complexities of raising children solo.

Shits and Giggles – Screw Burnout!

Burnout doesn't have to be the end of your story—it can be the beginning of your biggest transformation. Shits and Giggles – Screw Burnout! takes you on a humorous, no-nonsense journey to understand and conquer burnout. Monya Maxwell offers practical tools, real-life insights, and a hefty dose of self-compassion to help you reclaim your spark, refuel your energy, and get back to living the life you deserve. Say goodbye to burnout and hello to your comeback. It's time to put yourself first—no guilt, no shame.

Closing the Book – The Art of Emotional Evolution

This deeply personal visual and written journey explores the emotional terrain of healing, self-discovery, and letting go. Closing the Book is not a story of victimhood, but a testament to resilience—the courage it takes to face your pain, do the inner work, and step into your own light. Through evocative imagery and heartfelt reflections, Monya invites readers to witness a quiet yet powerful transformation: from holding on to finally letting go.

Coming soon.

www.ingramcontent.com/pod-product-compliance
Lightning Source LLC
Chambersburg PA
CBHW050330010526
44119CB00050B/734